G000245462

Spiritual
COMBAT
ACCORDING TO
ST BENEDICT

—

BERNARD DUCRUET, OSB

Translated by Giles Conacher OSB,
monk of Pluscarden Abbey

All booklets are published
thanks to the generosity of the supporters
of the Catholic Truth Society

TRANSLATOR'S DEDICATION:

To Ian McCafferty, who, besides French,
taught me more important things.

All rights reserved. First published 2022 by The Incorporated
Catholic Truth Society, 42-46 Harleyford Road, London SE11 5AY
Tel: 020 7640 0042. Copyright © 2022 The Incorporated Catholic
Truth Society. www.ctsbooks.org

ISBN 978 1 78469 741 9

Contents

Spiritual Combat: Translator's Introduction

Christian spiritual combat goes back to the very beginning, when "Michael, the prince of the heavenly host" did battle with the devil and his angels. In the last book of the Bible – Revelation, or The Apocalypse – the devil, the great red dragon, opposes the Woman clothed with the sun, crowned with twelve stars – Mary, Mother of God, and also of the Church. Still today the devil goes about like a roaring lion, seeking whom he can devour, opposing God and trying to subvert his Kingdom, tempting us and trying to prevent our reaching eternal happiness with God.

The Book of Job says that our life "is a soldiery on this earth" (*Jb* 7:1). St Paul tells the Ephesians, and us, "We are not contending against flesh and blood, but against the principalities, the powers, the world rulers of this present darkness, against the spiritual hosts of wickedness in the heavenly places" (*Ep* 6:12).

St John Cassian teaches:

> In order to achieve competence, in every profession, every art invented by human ingenuity, you need a master's teaching. So a guide is necessary for that invisible and hidden discipline, which is only accessible to the perfectly pure heart, in which mistakes do not lead to easily repaired material damage but to the loss of the soul and eternal death.

> Take note: here we are not confronting visible enemies, but ruthless invisible ones. It is a combat that goes on day and night, a spiritual combat; and not just against one or two enemies, but against countless legions; it is a combat of which the result is very much in doubt, if we consider how relentless is the enemy, and how stealthy are his attacks.

If you want to win, whether in war or athletics, you need discipline and sacrifice. Think of the almost obsessive efforts required of a top athlete, hours in the gym, the pool and on the track, endless exercises, careful diet, constant coaching – all for maybe ten seconds of glory… It's the same for soldiers: all that boring, repetitive training, relentlessly obeying orders, submitting to discipline, learning teamwork, trusting others, mutually supporting each other.

Finding the right coaches, trainers, is crucial. From experience they can teach you how to do it, point out your weaknesses and offer remedies, teach you routines, so that when the struggle comes, you are ready for it. In baptism the faithful are anointed with oil, to make them slippery customers in their wrestling with the enemy, supple in their athletic strivings.

Not surprisingly, Christianity has its coaches and trainers for our lifelong combat. Our friends and guides are the angels and saints. We have our personal bodyguard, our guardian angel, our friend who helps and guides us. All the angels and saints love and care for us, are interested in us, help us, and are very willing to assist when called. Some of them are specialists, and it is worth knowing their stories and skills – for gamblers, St Camillus is the one; he was addicted to gambling. Read their biographies; St Gregory the Great says that the lives of good people make lively and life-giving reading, and it's true. Anyone engaging in warfare or battle seeks allies to help in the struggle.

Prayer is essential for the combat. How? There is the *Our Father*, the prayer Jesus taught his disciples. Like his Mother Mary, like Joseph, like the Apostles, Jesus learned to pray through the Psalms. They are for us, too, on their own or in the Liturgy of the Hours, the Divine Office. Ask Mary's prayers, say the *Hail Mary*; it concludes, "pray for us...now and at the hour of our death" – that's pretty good, knowing that the Mother of God is praying for me right now!

St Benedict at the beginning of the Prologue to his Rule speaks of military service and the powerful and glorious weapons of obedience, wielded in the service of Christ the true King, and he offers some short combatants' prayers, reduced to a series of initials on his medal; their meaning is as follows:

TVRSNSMV: Go away, Satan, never persuade me with your empty suggestions;

SMQLIVB: The things you offer are evil, drink your own poisons;

CSSML; May the holy Cross be my light;

NSDMD; Let not the devil lead me.

We can learn these by heart, and add them to our prayer resources, whether for use in temptation or just generally.

A daily renewal of our baptismal promises – which include renunciation of the devil and his works – sharpens our purpose, puts a new edge on the weapons of our spiritual combat.

St Francis de Sales, that gentlest of shepherds, carried in his pocket a book by Lorenzo Scupoli, *Unseen Warfare*, and read it every month. That is another lesson we could usefully learn from this Doctor of the Church. It's a practical and helpful book.

When we read our Bible, it can help to have a goal. If we keep an eye out for passages referring to virtues we want to foster or vices we want to fight, we can note them, have them ready for use, a bit like fire-extinguishers – red for paper or cardboard, a black, carbon-dioxide extinguisher for the chip-pan. When tempted, reach for an appropriate Scripture extinguisher.

We need to keep an eye on what's going on in our hearts by examination of conscience – concentrating on a particular aspect, or just keeping an eye on trends. St Aloysius Gonzaga, who died aged 23, used to examine his conscience every 30 minutes. Excessive? But he did become a saint! Today we'd call it real-time monitoring.

Keeping an eye on the thoughts and impulses which come into our hearts or knock on the door is a 24/7 occupation. It's the virtue which the desert Fathers and Mothers call "watchfulness", and good sentries are an essential part of spiritual combat.

Abbot Bernard wrote this little book and led his community by word and example for twenty years; this is his wisdom, for you. Last of all, never despair of the Divine Mercy!

Giles Conacher OSB

Introduction: St Benedict

St Benedict was born at Nursia, a hundred kilometres north of Rome, about 480, and died at Monte Cassino in Campania around 547. His life unfolded in troubled times: the Roman Empire was assailed by successive waves of invaders from the east from 450 onwards.

At the end of the century Italy was conquered, bit by bit, by Theodoric, king of the Ostrogoths. Then the Byzantines came ashore at Naples in 536 and recaptured Rome. The following year the Goths once more besieged the city, and ten years later, about a year before Benedict's death, Rome was definitively conquered by the Gothic king Totila.

It was in this difficult political context, while armies came and went around the foot of Monte Cassino, that Benedict, withdrawn from political life, founded an oasis of peace and gathered a community in which patricians and slaves, Romans and Barbarians, the illiterate and scholars, together lived the peace of the Gospel. Benedict passed on to his community an art of living and a wisdom of love which he codified in a Rule.

When commenting on this Rule, which became the patrimony and common property of Europe, we usually think about St Benedict's wisdom. From the seventh century onwards, the Rome-based civilisation which flowed out from the monasteries covering Europe, from the Danube to the North Sea, from the Ebro to the Elbe, discovered in the Benedictine Rule its chief inspiration, its best concrete example of living out the Gospel, in a living-out in which economic life, liturgical life, relationships and personal life were all balanced in order, proportion, wisdom, respect for the human person and a solid belief in the primacy of God's service.

It was this aspect of Benedict's wisdom which led Pius XII in 1947, St Paul VI in 1964 and finally St John Paul II to choose him as principal Patron of all Europe (St John Paul II later added S Cyril and Methodius [followed by others including St Catherine of Siena and St Teresa Benedicta of the Cross, Edith Stein]).

But it is not under this aspect that we are going to study St Benedict's message. For St Gregory, when telling the story of Benedict's life in the second book of his *Dialogues*, describes him as a man who had received the gift of wisdom from his youngest years, living with the Spirit of all the just. But he insists on one charism which was particularly his: the discernment of spirits.

Benedict, who had himself found peace through his own life-long combat, animated his monastic sons' combat and helped them to find peace and communion, after having exorcised the devils which tempted them. If the monastery became a place of peace, harmony and serious work in every sphere, it was thanks to this unremitting spiritual combat led by Benedict in order to free his sons from all that got in the way of their openness to receiving the Spirit of Christ and the gift of charity.

The Spiritual Combat

In Eastern Christian monasticism, St Basil of Caesarea emphasises fraternal communion. From the beginning of his Rule, he puts before his disciples this charity in communion. Nowadays, the new communities very often give primacy to this aspect of the common life.

St Benedict, following the Fathers and Cassian, suggests the spiritual combat as what defines monasticism. Spiritual combat defines the monk and describes his life, from the very first chapter of the Rule.

The cenobite is one who "does battle under a rule and an abbot". The hermit is one who, "well prepared for the single combat of the desert by his training in the fraternal ranks, is henceforth strong enough, without anyone else's support, to do battle on his own, with God's help, against the vices of the flesh and thoughts".

So spiritual combat establishes the monk in his identity. Fraternal communion is the result of ascesis, and, as St Benedict described it at the end of his Rule, is a wonderful gift. In St Thérèse of Lisieux we find the same progression:

in Manuscript C she sings of her discovery of charity, which thereafter was no longer something she just practised, but a gift of God.

The Nature of Spiritual Combat

The most natural movement, the most natural motive force of our lives, is love for self, flowing out into love of others and of God, the most desirable good to acquire for our own flourishing. But that self-love is perverted when, swollen up, it turns back into itself as the only good, and empties out every other love: God and others. That is egoism.

Spiritual combat demands that we renounce this idolatrous "me" in order to seek the true God. The whole Gospel invites us, following Jesus, to crucify this swollen false relationship so that we may rediscover the wisdom of love. We have to lose ourselves so as to win ourselves, to go beyond ourselves to love, to renounce self in order to go to the other.

The Three Breaches

Our nature, with its needs and desires, is weakened by three tendencies which are like three breaches in our defences, three wounds which have remained open since the beginning. Today, many theologians apply themselves to justifying our belief in the mystery of original sin through learned commentaries on the first chapters of the Book of Genesis. But original sin is primarily an existential fact:

we all know by experience how we are weakened by these
three tendencies which we are now going to try to describe.

The first breach

The first breach in our defences is opened by covetousness,
which causes a weakening of the natural and healthy desire
for life, to exist, to produce, to beget. It is the perverse
tendency to grab for oneself, to possess for self, to create
and beget for the self. The desires for the Good and for
Goodness become the desire for well-being, to be as
comfortable as possible. That is the practical materialism
of one who no longer has any taste for prayer – *his belly
is glued to the earth*, says the psalm. He is afraid of any
effort involving going out from himself and going towards
others. The symbol of this covetousness is the pig, rooting
with his snout, constantly seeking what he can eat.

Fears of lacking or losing something, avarice, have
a tendency to graft themselves onto this. The search
for personal gratification arouses jealousies, envies,
resentments, with their following of lies and violence.

The Fathers speak of the three-fold covetousness for
money, sex and the world, with their perverse tendency
to centre everything on self. This covetousness is so
much *crouching at our door and lying in wait* for us, as
Genesis puts it, that even our most generous and altruistic
intentions are often mixed with hidden motivations rooted
in this very covetousness.

In combat we need to watch out for the very first covetousness-driven movements of our thoughts. But this does not mean denying the natural needs of our nature, nor even of the necessity of the pleasure that moves us. Our combat consists of redirecting our desire into becoming a sacrificial, offering attitude. That is what St Augustine describes as the Passover of our desire, crossing over from *cupiditas*, cupidity, to *caritas*, charity.

Because, for St Augustine, there is no question of devaluing or condemning pleasure; he wants to convert it, reconnect it with its source, direct it. Further, this Passover of our desire is not to be sought in any particular moment of our lives; it is a constant movement which represents the dynamo driving the whole of our human lives. Thus our life is "drawn by the desire for God to pass from Babylon to Jerusalem, from the old man to the new man, and from Adam to Christ, from non-being to true being".

The second breach

Desire's second breach in our defences plugs into our natural and healthy desire to be recognised and loved. For indeed, it is in recognition and love by others that our human nature as men and women is built up. We have need of all that ties us to our family, our relations, our culture, the education we have received, and so on.

It is within this nature, formed by a whole environment, that we discover what it means to be a "person", that deeper

"I" capable of entering into a personal relationship with the other. It is in order to discover and expand this personal "I" that the Bible gives us a commandment: that of leaving father and mother to be united in a personal relationship with your wife. It is what God says to Abraham: "Leave your country, your family, and go where I shall tell you to go" (*Gn* 12:1). Henceforth, Abraham would have a relationship of obedience with God, an altogether personal relationship, in trust and faith.

The perverse tendency which dwells within us is to divert this need to be known and loved to our sole profit. We then forget to go beyond it, so as to turn it into a true and personal relationship with the other. We sink it into the desire to be admired, exalted, well-thought-of, esteemed by those around us, in the desire to be widely-reputed, solely for our personal profit.

Such is the vanity of one who is always seeking a new pedestal, so as to be admired by a new set of onlookers. Here the image of the pig is replaced by that of the peacock, displaying itself; the swollen belly becomes the puffed-out chest.

Vanity then becomes the powerful motor of all we do. Our actions, even the most noble and heroic, are to a greater or lesser degree stained by that vanity of putting on a show, attracting attention and affection. John points this out in his Gospel, speaking of the Pharisees: many were beginning to believe in Jesus, but that faith was mixed up with the desire to be glorified by men. That vanity paralysed their efforts.

The spiritual combat here consists in redirecting this desire to be recognised. For there is a right attitude, that of Jesus praying to his Father to be glorified: "Father, glorify me so that I in turn may glorify you" (*Jn* 17:1). There is a love, a glory, a holiness for which we must thirst. But we are not going to seek it from men. God alone can glorify us. The saints are people who have been able to transform their vanity through this desire to be glorified by the holiness of God.

The third breach

The third breach which weakens us and makes us vulnerable to temptation slips itself into the healthy need to create, to organise, to control time and things. The perverse tendency consists of wanting domination over everything for the self, through power, riches or knowledge. So we seek as much influence and as wide an audience as possible. We try to keep the initiative in what happens, in things, in people, in ourselves, to make everything subject to ourselves.

We are the ones who are always right, who have the last word, who never recognise our faults or errors, never ask pardon. Here the eagle, which wants to rise far above everything else, is the symbol. "Me" becomes the idol. We think we are the best, believe that everything should be with reference to us.

This final perverse tendency, then, is that of pride. The Fathers say it is the pattern, the form, of all the other perversions. It shows itself in the desire to be totally autonomous, totally independent of all higher authority, whether of God or others.

But the spiritual combat can redirect this tendency by putting it at the service of the kingdom of God, rather than my own empire. Many saints and founders succeeded in converting their imperious spirit, to put it at the service of God.

To Sum Up

The desire which is based on natural needs – for security, to be loved and acknowledged, of being in the place where we belong – has unfortunately gone astray and is drawn to realisation of "me", the self. It becomes perverted, because instead of being directed to the Absolute Good which it would find in God, it turns in on itself by becoming pleasure-seeking, pursuing vanity and domination.

This deviation, this going astray, is original, as we see in the first narratives in Genesis. Jesus himself was tempted to seek self-realisation independently of God, tempted in those areas of weakness shared by every human – by the desire to be secure against lack of food, by the vanity of performing a great miracle in the sight of all the crowds in the temple, so as to be recognised, and finally, by the desire to dominate and rule the world.

But Jesus closed the door to those perverse tendencies because he was constantly with his Father and obeyed his Word. In us, the door is always more or less half-open, and through it the tempter bursts in with his suggestions, unless we remain watchful.

To the extent that we try to be honest with ourselves, we can only admit that the whole of our lives, including our noblest actions and deepest desires, are mixed up with the darnel of this self-seeking tendency under the three elements of thirst for pleasure and riches, the quest for honours, and power-seeking.

According to St Augustine, the whole of the spiritual combat consists not so much in killing desire, which is what drives our lives, but in redirecting it. Desire's perversity lies in its wish to turn itself away from God, to have no need of him, to be self-sufficient, to struggle against creaturely limitation and death, through possession of things and laying hold of the universe.

Because desire is radically limitless, in its "capacity for God" in its most positive form, so also it is limitless in its greed and in its search for fleeting and partial pleasures, for riches, honours, power, carnal pleasure. Their possession is never sufficient and is always compromised. This insatiable greed becomes a slavery, to the extent that we are possessed by the things which we think we possess.

This bondage is, according to St Augustine, the existential condition of life here below. Pride and greed engender ignorance, in other words lack of knowledge of self and the Creator, which brings about the inability to discern the beauty and order of creation and the world. This elicits the cry in the *Confessions:* "Where was I when I sought you? You were there in front of me, but I was far from myself, and I could no longer find myself, so much less could I find you."

Through spiritual combat, by risking losing ourselves, by opening ourselves to God and submitting to him, we recover our freedom. By recognising God as our Creator, we rediscover the meaning of our own existence. We can authentically love ourselves with the same love with which we love God. More radically still, we attain to the fullness of our humanity by allowing ourselves to be divinised:

> What you love, that you are. Do you love the earth? You shall be earth. Do you love God? You shall be God. What am I saying? Will you be God? I dare not say so myself, but let us listen to the Scriptures: *'I have said you are gods, you are all children of the Most High'.* (St Augustine).

This de-centring of desire is a Passover. We must die to the desire that is proud, grasping and vain, to open ourselves to the life-giving dynamism of charity, to the humble desire detached from self, which is the gift of the Spirit. This work of death and rebirth is the work of charity, for, as St Augustine once more says, "Those who have charity are born of God." We owe this victory to Christ, "who has come down to us, he who is our life, he took upon himself our death, he killed it by the superabundance of his life." Thus, it is by sharing in the death and resurrection of Christ that we can die to carnal desire and open ourselves to desire of the Spirit. This Passover is then "a passage from love of self and things, even to despising God, to love of God, even to despising self." It is the crossing over from illusion to true existence, from desire to possess God to accepting being possessed by him.

Conditions Which Worsen the Spiritual Combat

The Context

Our spiritual combat can be weighed down and handicapped by conditions, of which the first is our social environment. For example, our family may have marked our childhood with a certain pride, or avarice or class-based vanity. By imitation, that environment sets up in us a certain "super-ego", which strengthens our original self-centredness, which we are only too ready to cultivate.

Further, the whole of our culture – national, tribal, continental or ancestral – can condition our view of ourselves, exalting it, stimulating it, or, on the contrary, tangling it up psychologically. For example, there is a Western superiority-complex, and an altogether French vanity which is completely unbearable to foreigners [this is written by a Frenchman].

Even our religious community can worsen these various original tendencies: the tendency to possess, to seek to dominate, or to believe that we are better than others. It is good to be aware of all the influences which come to us from our environment, while at the same time avoiding projecting our own tendencies onto others.

In our western countries, a whole anthropology centred on man reinforces our self-preoccupation. It thinks of man independently from God, whether this be the radical view of atheism, or more subtly, as a belief in man complete in himself, self-sufficient and independent. Any other view is ruled out of court, as unscientific and therefore unacceptable.

But in either case we completely lose the reality of the fundamental relationship between man and God, and we are far from the thought of "man-made-for-God" which is at the heart of the thought of the Fathers, particularly St Augustine: "you have made us for yourself, Lord, and our heart is restless until it rests in you."

This modern western world-view, fostered by its effectiveness in dominating the world, also goes on to strengthen that perception of "me", of the self, which is so attracted by the temptation of prideful independence.

While on the subject of this influence, it is also necessary to mention taking part in certain associations involved in poorly understood far-eastern practices, in magic, drugs, alcohol, sexual depravity. Some sects tend to foster the desire to live for self, to aim at fulfilment for the self which seeks pleasure, vanity and domination.

To these exterior factors have to be added all the emotional injuries and traumas. These can make watchfulness difficult for some, and prevent them redirecting their desires. They cause attitudes of flight, violence, compensation and hardening to take root in the personality, closing the door to an attitude of self-giving, of offering, which is the only way of submitting the "I", the self, to the will of God and his love.

These wounds may arise from our family situation in our childhood or from events in the course of life which have, as it were, damaged our sensitivity. This has as a result become weakened and sickened, incapable of that watchful attention which is, as we shall see, essential for redirecting our desires.

The Dragging Dead-weight and Grace

By analysing all the conditions which make the spiritual combat harder, we might be tempted to think that the battle is lost before we begin, and that our freedom, so essential for this combat, is purely illusory. For – let us continue down this path – we are born without having been consulted on the matter: we have no choice about our parents, our country, our race, the historical epoch in which we live, our sex, our religion, etc. So we are prefabricated beings, as much in our physical as in our moral, psychological or affective being. We are prisoners of our biology, just as much as we are of our social environment.

But that is not our faith and our experience. We know that as human beings we are capable of refusing all that is contrary to our existence, to let ourselves be re-created by grace, beginning with that "I" which is much deeper than the biological and social "me". Because that much deeper heart than our sentient heart is indwelt by a love. Whoever knows they are loved by God can overcome all the dead-weights of physical nature and social being. We can take on trials, temptations, evil, sickness and even our sin.

The devil himself cannot reach that fundamental freedom we have, to respond to the grace of God, which ceaselessly invites us to arise and come back to the Father.

The Adversary

The kind of self-centred egoism we have described is so opposed to the true love of self, which radiates into personal relationships and self-giving to others, that it supposes not just the three original breaches in our nature, but also the perverse influence of the tempter.

He makes use of all the resources of our contemporary culture, of every event and every person, using them as his agents to widen the breaches and try to steepen the slippery slope which leads to self-destruction of the person. In her little book on the indivisibility of love, Madeleine Delbrel is not afraid to say, "The spirit of evil is not an idea; we must take seriously what Jesus says about him: that is Gospel realism. The spirit of evil is a tempter, he is not a 'temptation', he is 'prince of this world'."

In the Bible he has something like a hundred names, but he is mostly called the liar, the divider, the devil, the adversary. He is most seen in the Gospel, because the presence of Jesus forces him to reveal himself. He is someone, he is intelligent, but he is not a person, because as Cardinal Ratzinger says, he is the "anti-person", the "non-person". He breaks up and destroys personal being; in him there is nothing of love or unity.

Since he is beautiful, he attracts and seduces, but his work is accusation, suspicion, destruction. Brilliant, he disintegrates and destroys, and is the opposite of light, which illuminates and warms. He tempts and misleads – especially the holy – and sometimes possesses. He deceives, worries, divides, separates from God and others. He fosters interior murmuring, which divides the heart against itself. He is the "father of lies" and the "mystery of iniquity".

His main effort is directed to making us lose trust in God, to make us suspicious that God is jealous of our freedom and capacity to love. This fundamental fear of a God, whom he presents to us as "sadistic", he subtly mixes up with all the other fears which conceal this one. Thus, Adam replies to God in paradise, "I was afraid, because I was naked, and I hid myself" (*Gn* 3: 10); and we, too, out of a fear born of all our poverty, powerlessness and weakness, conceal a much more essential fear, of a jealous and vengeful God – an image planted in us by the adversary. Equally, the fear that the devil is everywhere is a temptation which paralyses us by preventing us from knowing God in truth and trusting in him.

But the adversary, prince of this world, does not act in hearts alone. He also acts in the history of the world, as Madeleine Delbrel also says:

> An intelligent spirit, by slipping himself into human affairs, he does so in such well-calculated doses that he manages to cause love and hate, pride and self-abnegation, murder and sacrifice to coexist and dwell together. He makes constant efforts to project onto every age, epoch and civilisation, a film of his world.

However, it is in the desert and in fervent communities that his action is most easily spotted. The cloister which separates us from the prevailing culture (in other words from this "world" in which he hides without anyone noticing), the vows which close up the breaches of desire and redirect them, and the organisation of the community around the just commandment of charity, all those force him out into the open.

In a climate of charity, it is much easier to identify anything rooted in lies, fear, acedia, presumption, jealousy, suspicion, accusation, murmuring, laziness, blindness, scorn, self-content, bitterness, avarice, intense agitation etc., and even more, of course, of pride, vanity and covetousness.

In the world, the evil spirit is not easy to distinguish, so greatly are anguish, disquiet and alienation prevalent in a universal evil. We do not know where to begin to combat it. In a community or a fervent heart, the least breath of the tempter, opposed to the Spirit of Charity, is immediately detected, identified and combatted.

The Desert Fathers liked to express this by saying that, in a city, a single devil with folded arms complacently watches the agents acting on his behalf, the places which engender vice or injustice and the natural-downward slide of every self-seeking person. Whereas in the monastery, a hundred devils strive to tempt the monks.

In his history of St Benedict, St Gregory the Great tells that not all monks possess the gift of discernment of spirits. Benedict had that charism, but his disciple Maurus only discerned the tempter after several days of fasting, while the monastery's superior, Pompeianus, could not make out why one poor monk was always dodging away from prayers.

Is St Benedict just a good psychologist? Psychologists observe character faults; the charismatic discerns the breath of the tempter. In order to cure the person, they need to work together.

Lastly, let us remember that the devils remain submitted to God's sovereignty. The book of Job teaches us that God makes use of their "ministry", but ultimately the enemy is always fighting against himself, because the elect emerge from the combat strengthened.

All the same, as God has given existence to the devils, they have complete freedom of choice and strategy, so that their perverse action in the world and history remains unforeseeable and subject to sudden new developments which keep us on our toes until the end of time, as the book of the Apocalypse (Revelation) shows us.

This is why humanity's slow progressive climb towards the noosphere [the realm of pure thought] described by Teilhard de Chardin in *Le Milieu Divin* is scarcely perceptible in the history of events, which often seems to move backwards.

Often temptation arouses us through struggle to a greater faith and greater trust in God, upon whom we fervently call in prayer. But we know, as St Paul says, that God never allows us to be tried beyond our strength. Through prayer, we ask him to chain the adversary to the foot of the Cross of Jesus, whose Name alone is enough to terrify hell.

Place of the Spiritual Combat

It is clear that the spiritual combat is waged on all fronts where conditions exist which lead to, exalt and stimulate the disintegration of our personal being and the idolatry of "me". Thus every kind of struggle against poverty, sickness, injustice, loneliness, the wrong kind of sorrow, hunger, nakedness and want has a spiritual dimension, and is not confined to the material and bodily.

Thus spiritual combat has medical, social, political and educational aspects. We must constantly say "no" to suffering in order to relieve it, to sickness in order to cure it, to every kind of sorrow, in order to offer consolation.

Humanity's combat to free itself from every kind of deprivation so as to give glory to God in whose image it is made is the Church's combat; it is also that of our families, whether natural or religious, striving to discover the unity of charity. It is also to be found in our own hearts, which need constantly to be reunified in love.

Still more for the monk, the battlefield is his heart. That is where he discovers the roots of doubt, despair, indifference, violence or hatred; he has to turn his heart round, redirect it, so as to find hope and peace. This personal combat offers an example to the Church and humanity.

The whole of monastic asceticism has as its goal being able to dwell in the depths of the heart, where God's presence dwells. We have constantly to move from our sensitive heart, the place of temptation, to the depths of our heart, where love enlightened by reason is docile to the lights and motions of the Spirit.

To "dwell in love", according to St John, is the fruit of grace and a gigantic combat, as the Fathers say, Isaac the Syrian among them.

Thérèse of Lisieux tells how, from the ages of 4 to 14 years she dwelt in her sensitive heart, where she was tempted by vanity or despaired of being loved. But one Christmas day, grace strengthened her, and for the next ten years she made giant strides in trust and love.

Main Principles of Spiritual Combat

So as not to lose confidence, and to bring our spiritual and social combat with evil to a successful end, we need to keep in mind some principles which will help us to achieve this. We will mention five of them here.

Seek Charity

The first principle is that when we are moved by the love of charity, we are not under the influence of the evil spirit and his suggestions. Another quotation from Madeleine Delbrel: "In his light–darkness combat Jesus uses love alone. St John, who grasps most forcefully the drama of light and darkness, is the only one who enters into it, and by love." It is a matter, therefore, of letting ourselves be constantly and ever more inspired and animated by the Spirit of Christ, for where the Holy Spirit is, the spirit of evil cannot be.

Spirit of God or Spirit of Evil?

The second principle is that there is nothing in common between the action of the Holy Spirit and that of the evil spirit. That spirit always acts from outside, and through the senses. Even when he reaches more deeply into our feelings through the emotions, then takes over the imagination through troubling images, finally managing to paralyse the intelligence, darkening and deceiving the judgement, we can always by *anamnesis* (spiritual remembering and enlightened discernment, often with another's help) work out the door through which on some occasion we consented to let him in, by accepting his suggestions.

But he can never go so far as to reach the freedom of the depths of our heart. On the contrary, the Holy Spirit, the creator of our freedom, operates in the depths of our hearts without taking us over or forcing us. His peaceful action pacifies, purifies, enlightens and builds up.

Sharing in the Redemption

A third consideration can help us in our combat. Our combat always shares in the task of Christ's redemption. With him, we battle and suffer to free others and all humanity. We need to make use of all our weaknesses, limitations, errors and temptations, and even our sin which humiliates us, in order to cling more closely to Christ and to allow ourselves to be reconciled by him. Thus we can draw a greater good from evil, for "everything works for the good of those who love God" (*Rm* 8:28). St Paul says further, "I am content with weakness, insults, hardships, persecutions and calamities for Christ, for when I am weak, it is then that I am strong" (*2 Co* 12:10). This power, this strength, is the very power of God within us, replacing our own, on which we can no longer rely.

Growth in Love

A fourth certainty must give life to our combat. That is the fact that ultimately the most usual result of our combat is a strengthening of our theological virtues of faith, hope and love, and through them a closer union with God, even if this is in the night of the senses and the soul. So, when we cry out, "O God, come to my aid, make haste to help me", this cry, bit by bit, intensifies our love of God, and causes it to descend ever more deeply into our hell.

A Battle of the Church

Lastly, we need always to be convinced that this combat is of the Church. The devil wants us to despair, by isolating us in silence and trying to persuade us that since we are on our own, we are bound to be overcome by our trials. But our combat is always in solidarity with, united to, every combatant in the Church. We are in communion with those who are undergoing the same trial. We suffer trial and temptation with and for the Church. We are cured in the Church, by her and for her. We do battle for, with and within the Church.

Chief Means of Spiritual Combat

All the means are given to us so that, united to Christ, we may rediscover a filial trust in God with an ever-increasing desire to find in him our fulfilment in peace and joy. We shall highlight five means used by different spiritual families, each of which, while not neglecting the other, lays greater emphasis on one aspect.

Prayer

The first means, which is universal, is prayer. When Jesus teaches us the *Our Father*, he teaches us not to be self-centred, and to give God the holiness, the glory and the power that we have a tendency to seek for ourselves. He also teaches us the trust which is content with what is necessary for today, and forgiveness to dissolve away in our hearts all that is not love.

Further, the Church's holy liturgy is an effective way of purifying our thoughts, as Simone Weil, like so many others, was happy to demonstrate.

The whole of Tradition agrees that psalmody is a means for this combat. This prayer needs to be bodily – in other words, said aloud, not merely mentally – and to be accompanied by actions – prostrations, deep bows, fasting – because spiritual combat is also physical.

The Church

A second aspect of this combat emphasises the help of the Church, its sacraments and sacramentals. For all the sacraments immerse us in the death and resurrection of Christ, so as to draw us into his Passover, by means of active faith and thanks to the Epiclesis, the invocation of the Spirit, which in each sacrament draws down his presence and action. Through the sacraments we share in the salvation brought by Christ; and in the spiritual combat, the sacrament of penance or reconciliation has a special part to play.[1]

The Works of Charity

Another approach emphasises apostolic action and commitment to works of charity. For indeed, the gift of

---

[1] **Author's note:** On exorcism, remember that it should never be used unless the sufferer consents and is personally committed to engaging in the spiritual combat, especially that of prayer. Otherwise the devil will return with seven others, as the Gospel emphasises. The exorcist must teach his patient to pray, to go to confession, to do penance and take part in the life of his parish community. Exorcism for a fee smacks of magic, fraud and trickery. The exorcist receives his mission from the Bishop: you don't just decide to be an exorcist!

self in the service of others, in all its possible forms, fosters an attitude of self-giving and self-detachment which is the goal of the spiritual combat.

Contemplation

There is also the contemplative approach. This approach emphasises the prayer of intimate union with Christ and his mysteries through loving "obscure" contemplation. In that way it develops the theological life. St John of the Cross describes what he calls the anagogical movement (in other words, from below upwards) and emphasises it, because it is the most helpful way for the soul to conquer the movements of the vices. It does not involve a lot of thinking, but rather raising ourselves to God without delay, as soon as we feel the first assault of vice, by a movement of love and raising of the heart. St Thérèse constantly practised this movement of self-abandonment, in what she called her "little way".

One special aspect of this contemplative approach is the Marian way. Union with Christ is then deliberately brought about by Mary, in Mary, with Mary. And this way uses such practical means as the rosary and consecration to Mary. St Louis Marie Grignon de Montfort demonstrates the power of this devotion to the mystery of Mary in the spiritual combat. He describes it as a universal means, even if not everyone has explicit recourse to it. In the Apocalypse, St John describes for us the woman, who is a figure both of Mary and the Church, at the heart of the battle waged by the dragon.

Here we should make special mention of seeking to discern spirits through the methodical examination of the motives which lead us to act, or of the thoughts which come into our hearts, following the teaching of St Ignatius.

The Monastic Way

Let us conclude this listing of the Church's main traditional ways of successfully waging the spiritual combat by mentioning the monastic approach, which St Benedict in particular advocates. We could dwell on this at some length, but it will be enough to say a few words.

This way is that of humbly watching for the presence of God, together with laying open before our spiritual father all the thoughts and desires that arise in the heart. This way seeks to follow Christ more particularly on his path of obedience, which led him, by the way of self-emptying, to the glory received from his Father.

This monastic combat can lead to *apatheia*, in other words, the pacifying of all the passions, which are all thereafter directed towards God, purified of all pride, vanity or covetousness and submitted to the action of the Holy Spirit, to his lights, to his motions and to his graces of union. This way can be a community way, among the cenobites, or a solitary way, among the hermits.

Conclusion: Filial Spirit

Spiritual combat has as its most important result the rediscovery of that filial trust in God which grows ever more complete. St Benedict expresses this from the very beginning of the Prologue of his Rule:

> Listen, my son, to a master's invitation, and incline the ear of your heart; lovingly receive the admonitions of the father who loves you, and by your actions carry them out; so as to return by the labour of obedience to him from whom you separated yourself by the laziness of disobedience.
>
> To you therefore my discourse is now addressed, whoever you are, who are renouncing your own will to serve under the true king the Lord Jesus Christ, and take up the powerful and glorious arms of obedience.

As we have seen, each spiritual family emphasises one aspect or another, without, nonetheless, neglecting the others; we could also mention the role played in some cases by devotion to the angels or saints, or a specific aspect of the mystery of our faith – there is an infinite diversity of means to be found in the Church.

In the same monastery, each monk is free to nourish his soul according to his needs and spiritual tastes, for freedom is absolutely necessary for him. Alone before God, he can only be true by being himself and by following as faithfully as he can the action of the Holy Spirit in the secret of his heart. In the desert, there are scarcely any beaten tracks, nor landmarks. Each monk has quite quickly to abandon the conduct of his life to the Spirit, and to pursue the mystery which calls him to unknown and often unsuspected paths. St Benedict points out to us a way which he tells us is for beginners, then he leaves us with the Gospel, the Scriptures, the Fathers and the Holy Spirit.

But this way which the Rule offers us involves a deep experience of self, the true self, the "me" separated bit by bit from its masks, from its fears, become naked in its poverty and sin. Before its God who calls out to it, "Adam, where are you?" (*Gn* 3:9) it presents itself simultaneously as a criminal awaiting sentence and as a beloved child who leaps into its father's arms.

As the monk continues to climb the mountain of transfiguration, he constantly murmurs in his heart the Publican's prayer, "Jesus Christ, Son of God, have mercy on me a sinner" (*Lk* 18:18), a prayer which he sometimes transforms into: "Lord Jesus Christ, you are my joy, send forth your Spirit and save me."